Teen
Suicide

A Book For Friends, Family, and Classmates

Teen
Suicide

Janet Kolehmainen
and
Sandra Handwerk

Lerner Publications Company
Minneapolis

This book is available in two editions:
Library binding by Lerner Publications Company
Soft cover binding by First Avenue Editions
241 *First Avenue North*
Minneapolis, Minnesota 55401

LIBRARY OF CONGRESS CATALOGING-IN-PUBLICATION DATA

Kolehmainen, Janet.
  Teen suicide.

  Bibliography: p. 69
  Summary: Discusses what is known about suicide,
the myths, misconceptions, causes, and warning signs,
and uses hypothetical case studies to demonstrate
methods of prevention and coping with grief and guilt
after a suicide.
  1. Youth — United States — Suicidal behavior —
Juvenile literature. 2. Suicide — United States —
Juvenile literature. 3. Suicide — United States —
Prevention — Juvenile literature. 4. Loss (Psychology) —
Juvenile literature. [1. Suicide] I. Handwerk, Sandra.
II. Title.
HV6546.K65   1986   362.2   86-10333
ISBN 0-8225-0037-X (lib. bdg.)
ISBN 0-8225-9514-1 (pbk.)

Manufactured in the United States of America

  2 3 4 5 6 7 8 9 10 96 95 94 93 92 91 90 89 88 87

The authors would like to thank all the teenagers who shared their thoughts and feelings with us, especially Julie, and all the adults who have shown their concern for young people. Our special thanks to: Felicia, who suggested the project; Phil, who showed us the "magic" of computers; and Theresa Early, our editor, who gave so generously of her time and expertise.

Contents

CHAPTER ONE

What We Know About Suicide

Everyone has days when nothing seems to go right . . . and everything seems to go wrong. For most people, that feeling lasts only a short time, and then they breathe a sigh of relief and go on with living. For some people, though, the feeling that everything is wrong *doesn't go away*. Over time, they grow to feel empty and hollow inside. We've written this book for those of you who feel this way and for the friends and family of young people who experience these feelings. This book will tell you the specific warning signs of suicide you can watch for and actions you can take if need be. In this chapter, we will discuss teen suicide in general. In future chapters, we will give you the stories of typical cases and list possible ways for you to help someone in need.

How Great Is the Problem?

The Centers for Disease Control in Atlanta, Georgia, estimate that every year about 5,000 teens kill themselves and attempts may number 500,000. These figures are shocking, but even more horrifying is the possibility that someone you know might feel so desperate and lost that he or she would seek this end to pain. Numbers can't begin to measure the effects of a suicide attempt on family and friends. The victims of a teen suicide are not only the young person who dies, but the whole extended community in which that young person lived. The tragedy of a teen suicide is not only in the loss of a young person and his or her potential for contributing to society, but also the life-long grief felt by people who were close to the teen. We all need to educate ourselves and be ready to offer as much help as we can to prevent teen suicide.

Myths

People who try suicide are crazy.
Before doctors began to study teen suicide, most people thought that any young person who tried to die had to be insane. Now we know that this is

the greatest myth surrounding teen suicide. Teens come to consider suicide as their only option in much the same way adults would—only they may not know how to find help.

There *are* days when just about everything seems to go wrong, but most of us are able to get through the bad times with thoughts that things will get better. Some teens are not able to do this. Perhaps they can't believe that things will get better because they have already had a greater number of difficult things happen to them than would happen to most people in an entire lifetime (like death in the family, parents' divorce, breaking up with a girlfriend or boyfriend). Or perhaps the difficult things that happen to them cause them to feel very intense emotional pain. This long string of bad luck or this intense emotional reaction to problems is generally called "haplessness."

And some teens feel that they are unable to do anything to improve their situation. They may have tried everything they could think of and nothing has helped. Or they may just not know what to try. The important thing is that they feel they have no options. This feeling that they can do nothing to improve their lives is generally called "powerlessness" or "helplessness."

When someone has experienced these first two conditions, and has gone past the point at which he or she feels able to cope, that person may reach the last stage of despair—"hopelessness." He or she may attempt suicide at any point but an attempt is most likely to happen after the person has tried to cope, has felt unable to improve things, and has felt hopeless for a period of time.

Of course, some teens have a limited ability to cope. This might be due to the problems in their lives, or because they have not learned coping skills, or because of a true mental illness. Some young people experience horrible tragedy and continue to function, while others have difficulty handling the necessary experiences of growing up. The latter group of teens would reach the stage of hopelessness much more quickly than the former. We have, however, tried to describe the *average* teen who may attempt suicide.

People who talk about it, never really kill themselves.

Anyone who talks about suicide needs to be taken seriously and encouraged to seek help. Even those teens who talk about suicide as a way to shock or alarm parents and friends are asking for help. The teens who feel they must make such a dramatic threat in order to make someone care for them, or bother with them, need to learn why they feel as they do, and to find more effective ways to relate to others. Teens who talk about suicide will probably be most in need of professional help, and of support from family and friends. Most importantly, we need to listen to, and believe, anyone who tells us of his or her feelings.

Talking to teens about suicide will give them ideas about doing it.

Talking about suicide in an attempt to educate, or as a way to assess whether a teen will attempt suicide, will not give anyone the desire to commit suicide. Usually, thoughts of suicide develop over time. Suicide is seen as a last choice. Talking about suicide with teens who are seriously considering it may offer them the chance to express their feelings and to understand that they need help. When you talk about suicide, you offer a troubled young person the chance to ask for help.

Someone who is suicidal will never be "OK" again.

Suicidal thoughts are temporary rather than permanent. With professional help, a young person can replace feelings of hopelessness with positive attitudes toward life.

People who consider suicide may not be "crazy" but they are "different".

Another myth about suicide is that people who consider attempting it are somehow "different" from the rest of us. In fact, *anyone* who experiences great emotional pain may eventually consider suicide. For most young people, the pain in their lives never seems so acute and so never-ending that they are not able to go on. They can see the present experience as temporary. They can look to the future with hope. The person who considers suicide sees no possibility of an end to his or her pain.

Who Attempts Suicide?

The person who feels extreme emotional pain is the type of person who may consider suicide. However, this pain may be buried under an "I'm OK" shell which makes it difficult to see. Just as people show their happiness in many different ways, they also show their pain in many ways.

Teens who are "perfect" may be denying distress to others and to themselves. They may fill their time with over-achieving, with activities and with attempts to win the approval of others. These are attempts to feel less empty inside. These activities do not diminish their pain, they only make it more intense and less visible to others.

Teens who seem to be rebelling against everything may also be in great pain. These young people cover their pain and helplessness with anger. They may try to exert power over other people through anger and bullying because they feel they have no control over their own lives. Often, young people who become heavy users of drugs or alcohol are trying to forget their pain or get away from their unhappiness. The alcohol or drugs help them to feel different or to escape for awhile. Many times, a teen who uses drugs is feeling bad inside and trying to cope with things that seem unmanageable.

The key to suicide attempts is emotional pain. In some instances the pain builds over a period of time, while in others, it is an intense reaction to a particular event. While each case of suicide is highly individual, the common thread running through each story is a desperation to get away from an unusually high degree of emotional pain. Suicide can be considered the final step in trying to escape from overwhelming emotional agony.

Warning Signs of Suicide

If we are to understand how to prevent suicides or suicide attempts, we must all become familiar with the warning signs which may alert us to someone's pain and an impending suicide attempt. There are a number of ways in which teens may show they are considering suicide:

1) A previous suicide attempt

Anyone who has made a previous attempt at harming himself or herself is always considered at high risk of another attempt. Teens who are not sure of their decision to take their lives may lead up to a serious attempt at suicide by a series of increasingly self-destructive acts. In addition, anyone who has made an attempt at suicide and begins to speak again of his or her pain or of making another attempt should be taken seriously.

2) Talk or thoughts of suicide or death

Any time a teen begins to talk about suicide or seems to concentrate on thoughts of death, the situation may be critical. Although people may believe that teens use

threats of killing themselves to get attention or to shock
or "get their way," the possibility exists that they may
feel desperate enough to attempt or complete a suicide.
Their reasons are not what matters. All that will be
remembered is that the teens *did* harm themselves.
Remember, too, most of us are not in the position to
make professional judgments about the potential for
suicide, so any threat or discussion of suicide must be
taken seriously.

3) Changes in personality or mood

Teens are in the midst of immense physical and
psychological changes, so it may be difficult to tell if a
friend is just "down" or is in intense emotional pain.
But any change which seems to persist over time—either
depression or depression followed by elation—must be
taken seriously. This may be especially true if there
does not seem to be any reason for this change.

4) Changes in eating or sleeping patterns

Many people who are under stress respond with
changes in eating patterns (either eating more or less)
or in their sleeping patterns (either sleeping more, less,
or at different times than usual). Changes may be
noticeable at school, at home, or at work. For example,
you may realize that someone isn't eating, or you may
notice that he or she doesn't go with you to the lunch-
room, or that his or her clothes seem to be getting
baggy. The same may be true with sleeping. Your friend

may spend most of the time sleeping or complain about having insomnia and feeling exhausted all the time.

5) *Withdrawal from friends and activities*

Since friendships and activities are usually so important to teens, any change in involvement with either may signal real danger. The teen who suddenly seems to pull away from people or activities which previously gave pleasure may be telling us that he or she no longer has the energy required for this involvement. It is also possible that a young person who is feeling desperate will turn to other troubled teens. This might be an effort to find people who will "understand" his or her emotional pain.

6) *Taking unusual risks*

All teens take risks and that is part of learning about themselves. However, if teens begin to take risks which offer serious danger to themselves or others, we need to investigate why this is happening. The teen who has a series of "accidents" or the teen who drives reck-lessly may be signaling us that he or she holds little regard for life.

7) *Drug abuse*

This may include the overuse and abuse of both alcohol and other street or prescription drugs. Remember that use of any drug is an attempt to feel good or different. The teen who needs to artificially change the way he or she feels is in trouble. We need to look beyond the symptom of drug abuse to the cause.

8) *Final arrangements—giving away prized possessions, making peace with friends*

The teen who considers ending his or her life often makes arrangements for those things which are important to him or her to be distributed among friends, tells friends and family that everything is OK, or writes letters which explain why he or she has suicided. The teen who is ready to leave this life often feels he or she no longer has need for possessions, or must end attachments to family and friends.

The next chapters will present some situations which you may recognize as similar to situations that have occurred to you. While they seem realistic, the stories are not descriptions of real people. Rather, each story is a combination of several true stories and each character is a combination of several real people.

Each chapter ends with a discussion of the most important points about the situation presented in the chapter. We hope that this book will help you know when and where to seek help . . . either for yourself or for those around you who are crying out for help.

CHAPTER TWO

Steve

"Boy, this spring sure is different from last year!"

"Why?"

"Oh, a year ago I was this close to putting a bullet in my head." Steve held up his thumb and index finger just a little bit apart. "It's hard to believe now, but I sure was serious then."

Bob and Steve were stretched out on the fresh grass in the park, enjoying one of the first really warm afternoons of spring.

"Did you really want to kill yourself?" Bob asked.

"Well...maybe...no, not really. I just couldn't stand my life the way it was then. It's kind of hard to explain."

"Do you mind talking about it? I mean, I'm really curious," Bob said. "I've known you since last January and you've always seemed pretty stable to me." Bob and Steve were good friends now and Bob figured it was OK to ask. If Steve minded, he'd let him know.

"It's OK. For a while I couldn't talk about it at all,

but now I don't mind. It's just . . . I don't know if I can make you understand."

"Well, I don't know if you can either, but I've always wondered how a guy could think about dying on purpose. I always figured anybody who wanted to kill himself was just plain weird but if *you* were serious about it, I must be wrong. You seem pretty normal. I know suicide happens, but I don't know what leads up to it, or why, or stuff."

"Thanks for the vote of confidence! I *feel* pretty normal now, too. I don't know all of it myself—the why, I mean. Maybe I never will. I can tell you one thing, though—if I ever start feeling that way again, I'm going to talk to someone *fast!*"

Steve settled back on the grass. He wasn't sure that Bob would understand how he'd felt a year ago but he wanted to try to explain. He'd been thinking about it long enough. Now that he was OK, it might be interesting to try to explain to someone else, a friend, what it had been like a year ago. And maybe it would help him understand it better himself, and clear it out of his mind.

"It wasn't like I woke up one day and wanted to kill myself. It was much more gradual than that. I had a lot of problems back then. My grades weren't so good and I didn't qualify for the state track tournament. I know that happens to other people, but it was like I just ran out of steam. I just couldn't think of any way to make things better. It seemed like every day something else would go wrong or get a little worse and I was just *so tired*. Does that make any sense?"

"I guess so. But wasn't there anybody around— couldn't you talk to somebody?"

"Maybe I could have. But at the time, it didn't seem like it. I felt sort of invisible. I mean, everybody around me was busy with their own stuff, and I didn't think anybody really cared about my problems. My mom and dad were fighting all the time, my sister was working constantly, and my best friend spent all his time with his girlfriend. It was weird—I kept hoping that somebody would notice how bad I felt but I just couldn't say anything to anyone. I wanted to, but I was convinced that nobody had ever felt the way I was feeling, so nobody could understand."

Steve paused a minute. "I was scared, too."

"Of what?"

"That maybe I was nuts. Or so out of it that if I said something everybody would think I was a real freak. I couldn't take that."

"So what did you do?"

"Well, I was so sure that I was different from everybody else that I spent a lot of time alone. I pretty much avoided everybody unless it was absolutely necessary to be with them. I slept a lot—it seemed like being asleep was the only painless way to spend time."

"I've done that sleeping routine sometimes myself, but I wasn't suicidal. I mean, when I'm really bummed out I just go to sleep, and get a fresh start the next day."

"That's the way to do it," Steve agreed. "But the trouble was, I didn't get a fresh start the next day. Every new day was just as bad, to me, as the one before.

I really felt like I was at the bottom of a pit and I just couldn't get out. And there didn't seem to be anyone around who cared enough to help me."

"So is that when you started thinking about killing yourself?" Bob asked.

"You know, it's funny, but I don't think I actually ever *started* thinking about it. It was more gradual than that. I mean . . . I remember reading about suicides in the newspaper and thinking stuff like 'well, at least their troubles are over.' Then I started thinking that maybe if I were gone people would miss me. But most of all, I just wanted not to feel anything anymore because everything I felt *hurt*. And I was *so sick* of that."

"I still don't understand why you didn't tell somebody how you felt," Bob said.

"I tried, but I couldn't get the words out. I sort of hinted around that I was unhappy, but I just couldn't come out and tell anybody how bad it really was."

"Well, something must have happened. You're still here."

"I guess I got lucky. I had a cousin that I'd been real close to when we were little. I remember thinking that if I decided to kill myself, I'd like him to have my tape deck because he'd always said how great it was. So I wrote him a note and told him I wanted him to have it. I hadn't really decided how I was going to die. I was thinking about stuff like running the car in the garage with the doors shut, or maybe getting hold of a gun. Anyway, my cousin got real worried because he knew I loved that tape deck. He's a little older than me, and maybe that helped, but anyway, he called me up and asked me what was going on. I must have sounded strange because he called my parents and my friends and said he was really worried about me. He must've scared everybody because all of a sudden everybody was asking me how I felt and what was wrong and all that."

"Did you tell them?"

"No . . . at least not right away."

"So what happened?"

"Well, my cousin came over one night and started talking to me and asking questions and really listening to what I said. He didn't try to tell me I was wrong to feel the way I did or anything. He just more or less made me feel like he cared if I lived or died."

"Was that enough to make everything OK?"

"No, but it did make me feel a little better. At least someone was hearing me and I wasn't invisible anymore. My cousin finally convinced me to talk to the counselor at school. I didn't want to at first, but my cousin got me to see that I needed to talk to somebody, and I'd always trusted the guy at school so it seemed worth a try."

"What did the counselor do?"

"Well, my cousin had called him so he had an idea of what was going on. He was really great and listened to me. He didn't act as if I were crazy or anything. One thing he did, that I wasn't too happy about at first, was to tell me that my parents should know how I felt. He was OK, though, because he said he'd help me. He promised that if I talked with him every day, he wouldn't tell anyone at school what was going on. He *did* say that eventually I had to get some outside help from a counselor or somebody because he couldn't handle this by himself."

"How long did you see him?"

"About three weeks. Then he said he wanted to bring my parents in for a conference. That really freaked me out. I wasn't sure I was ready for that, but he said that I wasn't going to feel any better until my parents knew. I respected this guy, so I went along with him even though I didn't want to."

"What happened when he talked to your parents?"

"That was some conference! Mr. Andrews, the counselor, had me come to the meeting too. He was real calm. At first my parents were shocked and kind of half mad at what he was saying. It seemed as if they were embarassed at having a kid like me. But now I think they felt that my problems were their fault and that they weren't good parents. Mr. Andrews kept explaining that the important thing was to help me, not to look for someone or something to blame. He asked me if I'd see someone outside of school. Then he asked my parents if they'd go along with my decision.

"What did they say?"

"Well, my mom was sort of 'anti-shrink,' but Mr. Andrews was very firm about my needing someone to talk to, so she gave in. My dad didn't say much. He didn't seem too anxious to believe any of this, but he agreed to counseling. Mr. Andrews had a bunch of names of people we could contact."

"How long did you get counseling?"

"About eight months. I still see a therapist occasionally, and I can call him whenever I need to talk."

"So how are you now?"

"I'm fine. Things aren't perfect, but I understand a lot now that I didn't then. You know, last spring, when all this was happening, just feeling the weather get warm depressed me. It was like everything and everybody had something to look forward to—except me. Now I see the grass, and feel the sun, and I look forward, too. I haven't solved all my problems but I'm sure willing to hang around a while. I think my life will get better."

Steve got up and stretched. "Well, now you know my story. What do you think?"

Bob got up, too. "I'm glad you were willing to talk to me. I think I understand a little better, at least, how people feel when they think about suicide. I'm glad you don't feel that way anymore. I just wonder how many other people feel that way, but don't have a cousin or somebody who's smart enough to do something. I think that maybe I'll be a little more careful to notice if any of my friends get really down. And I hope I'll have guts enough to talk to them about what's wrong."

Steve smiled. "You know, sometimes, that's all it takes."

Listening and Caring

When people are seriously depressed it is difficult for them to discuss how they feel. Like Steve, they may only be able to "hint" at their unhappiness.

Unfortunately, that can make it hard for other people to notice their desperation. If you *do* become aware of the pain of a friend or relative, it is important that you make the effort to listen closely to what that person is saying. You don't have to argue or try to convince them to feel differently. Just try to let them know that you care that they feel so bad.

Accepting the Feelings of Others

When you think that no one understands how you feel, it's hard to talk. Someone who is suicidal feels isolated and "different." They may be reluctant to talk to you because they are afraid you will think they're "weird" or "crazy." They may not realize that we can't choose the emotions we feel, we can only choose how to act on those feelings. If you can show them you understand that they have these feelings and are not criticizing them, they may be willing to talk openly.

Unfortunately, your help may not be enough. When someone feels there are no choices left, other than to die, talking and listening may not convince them that they really want to live. In such circumstances, it is especially important that other people become involved in the problem.

CHAPTER THREE
Melissa's Problem

"Give me a *break!*"

Melissa slammed her locker shut and rested her forehead against the cool metal for a minute. The last few weeks had been horrible. Ann was so down that being with her made Melissa feel depressed—and worried. Ann just didn't have any energy anymore. Melissa sighed.

I know things are tough right now for you, Ann, she thought to herself, *but why can't you understand that it's bound to get better. Let's have a few laughs for a change!*

After supper that evening, Melissa went over to Ann's house, determined to cheer her up. "Hey, Ann, let's rent a movie and get a pizza later. We can put our feet up and pig out!"

"Oh, I don't know, Mel. I don't really feel up to it."

"Geez, Ann! What's the big deal about a movie and a pizza?"

"I don't know. I just can't get excited about anything. Maybe you should go home."

"No way! I'm going to cheer you up if it's the last thing I ever do!"

Ann sighed. "It's just . . . I'm so sick of everything going wrong. My grades are falling, mom and dad yell at me all the time, David never calls me anymore. Nothing good happens and I can't see anything changing."

"Gosh, Ann, I didn't know you felt *that* bad. But Christmas isn't too far off, maybe things will get better during vacation."

"I don't think so. Mel, I'm going to tell you something but you have to promise not to tell anyone else."

"I promise," said Melissa.

Ann hesitated before continuing, "I've been collecting my mom's sleeping pills, a few at a time. I've got about sixty now, and if things get any worse—I'm going to take them. It would be a relief not to have to get up in the morning."

Melissa didn't say anything but her eyes grew wide. Thoughts were chasing each other around in her mind. Soon she said she had homework, and left.

She didn't sleep well that night and couldn't concentrate in school the next day. The big problem was, she had told Ann she wouldn't tell anyone. But she didn't feel like she could do anything to help her friend by herself. What a mess!

At lunch she ran into Jean.

"Does Ann seem awfully down to you lately?" Melissa blurted.

"I'll say," Jean replied. She seemed relieved Melissa had asked. "I'm really worried about her but I don't know what to do. I'm afraid she may be thinking about killing herself!"

"Me, too. She's told me some things that really make me nervous but I told her I wouldn't tell anybody else. I don't know how to help her. What do you think we should do?" Just being able to say "we" made Melissa feel better. It was a relief to share her worries with someone else.

Jean said, "You know, we might go to Mrs. Flemming. She's Ann's favorite teacher and she seems pretty decent. We could just sort of ask if she has noticed anything."

Melissa wasn't sure about talking with an adult. You couldn't be sure that an adult would really listen to you and not go telling everyone else about Ann. "How about if we talk with a couple of other people first, and see if they think she's in trouble?"

"Yeah, OK. But I think we'd better talk to Mrs. Flemming, too. We can tell her we'd like her to keep this to herself. I know she's done that before with other kids. Why don't you talk to Bob, and I'll check with Don to see if he's noticed anything?"

"All right," Melissa said, "I'll do it after study hall."

The next morning Jean and Melissa compared notes. Both Don and Bob had said they had heard Ann talk about being a drag on everyone and not caring about anything any more. Before her first class, Melissa stopped by Mrs. Flemming's room and asked if she would talk to the girls after school that afternoon.

After the last bell, Jean and Melissa met and walked to Mrs. Flemming's room. Melissa still had second thoughts.

"Hello, girls. What can I do for you?" she greeted them.

"Well—ummm," said Jean, "we were wondering if you've noticed that Ann seems pretty down lately?"

"As a matter of fact, I've been concerned about her. Her grades are dropping. I know that my class is her favorite. Why do you ask?"

"Well . . ." Melissa had a hard time putting her fears into words. Finally she blurted out, "Mrs. Flemming, we're really worried about Ann but we need for you not to tell anyone else about this conversation. Can you do that?"

Mrs. Flemming frowned slightly, thought for a while and then said, "I can promise you that I won't repeat the conversation. But if Ann is really in trouble, I may feel that I have to discuss the situation with someone else. I wouldn't mention either of you. Will that be good enough?"

It wasn't exactly what Jean and Melissa wanted to hear, but it did make sense, so they agreed. They told Mrs. Flemming about their conversations with Ann, and Melissa told about the sleeping pills. Mrs. Flemming started pacing around the room.

"Girls, this could be very dangerous! We have no idea when or if Ann will take those pills. The first thing I want you to do is make sure Ann is *not* left alone. Go over to her house. Talk with her and listen to her. If she talks about suicide, let her. Don't argue about whether or not she ought to feel the way she does, just show her you care about her. I'm going to talk to a friend of mine who's a counselor and get some advice. After that, I'll talk to Ann myself. If you feel that she is about to take those pills, tell her parents or call me—no matter what time it is. I'll give you my home phone number."

Melissa objected. "Mrs. Flemming, we couldn't possibly tell anyone else about Ann. How would we know that Ann was about to take the pills? We especially couldn't go running up to Ann's parents!"

"Look, Melissa," Mrs. Flemming said, "the one thing you absolutely have to remember in a situation like this is that no matter how angry Ann might get, neither you nor she can afford to let her make a suicide attempt. If that means telling her parents, that's what you have to do! If she does make an attempt, you'd have a hard time forgiving yourself for letting it happen. It would be better to call someone, even if it's a false alarm, than to let it happen. Ultimately, you're better off, and so is she, if she's angry and alive—not dead."

As hard as it was for her, Melissa understood that Mrs. Flemming was right. It seemed pretty scary, though. She just hoped Mrs. Flemming could talk to her friend and get Ann some help before Melissa had to do something like telling Ann's parents!

Not Keeping Secrets

There are some secrets that are dangerous to keep. The burden of trying to help a suicidal person is a very heavy one and can't be managed by one person alone, no matter what his or her age. Sharing the problem is one of the first steps in getting help for someone who may be considering suicide. There may be several people who have noticed the changes in a friend's behavior that are signals of suicidal feelings. Unless they share their information, they may not realize that the possibility of suicide exists. In the story, Melissa was lucky that she spoke with Jean because she found out that other people were worried about Ann, too.

Involving an Adult

Like it or not, adults usually have more knowledge and "power" when it comes to dealing with a crisis like suicide than young people do. The adult who becomes involved may be of your choosing. It can be anyone you trust, for example: a parent, teacher, minister, family doctor, or just a close friend. If the first person you talk to seems unhelpful or unconcerned, keep trying. Find someone who will listen and do something.

It's fortunate that Mrs. Flemming was available to talk with Melissa and Jean. As an adult, Mrs. Flemming would be able to get expert advice, and to help the girls help Ann. Her suggestions were good ones. People who may be suicidal need desperately to know that someone cares about them. Because they already feel isolated from their family and friends, being alone can trigger an attempt on their lives.

Personal Limitations

Nobody's perfect! Each of us has limits in the amount of help we can give to other people. No one can live someone else's life for them, or take on the sole responsibility of keeping another person alive. At some times we can give more help than at other times. It depends on our own situation. It's extremely important for each of us to realize when we are "in over our heads." When that happens, we need help from other people, not only for our friend but also for ourselves. In the story, Melissa understood that she could not help Ann by herself. For her own protection, as well as Ann's, she needed to involve other people. Ann may feel that there is nothing to live for, but if she can be kept alive long enough to get some help, she'll have the chance to solve some of her problems and discover that death is not the solution she wants to choose.

CHAPTER FOUR

Why Didn't I Do Something!

That stupid jerk! I can't believe he'd do something that dumb!

Chris took a swing at the punching bag in his room. He was furious. And afraid. Tim had killed himself. Tim—who seemed so together. And Chris hadn't had any warning...or had he? Feelings of panic rose in Chris's chest.

How am I going to get through this? I did know—I did know and I didn't do anything. How am I going to live with that? Damn Tim! He had no right to do this to me!

He looked at his desk. Were the science fiction paperbacks Tim had given him a week ago a final present? His way of saying good-bye? Was Chris the only one Tim had given things to? Should he have known...?

Tim had been a really independent guy. He had had friends and done a lot of stuff at school, but he had always been his own person—quiet, controlled. Chris had liked that about him. He had been an easy guy to be around—he didn't demand too much. Which was fine with Chris because he sure had enough hassles in his own life—school, his parents, his girlfriend—all wanting too much from him. Was that why he hadn't noticed that Tim was in trouble until it was too late? Well, actually, he *had* noticed, but he had just been too busy to say anything. He had thought it could wait.

If I'd been a better friend, would he be alive today? Chris asked himself. The answer had to be at least a "maybe."

How am I going to live with this? Why didn't I do something?

Chris found himself reliving the weeks before Tim's death over and over again. He couldn't seem to concentrate on anything else. His grades began to drop and he had arguments with everybody around him. He felt so damned guilty! And it was getting worse, not better. What would people think if they knew he had known that Tim might kill himself? They'd think he was a lousy person, that's what they'd think. Maybe he ought to do what Tim had done...that might solve all his problems.

"Chris sure is hard to get along with lately!"

"Yeah, he's being a real jerk."

"I wonder what's bugging him?"

Chris's friends on the basketball team were confused. They were having a hard time getting along with Chris, who used to be a nice guy.

Even the coach had noticed the changes. One day in

practice it all seemed to come to a head. Chris practically screamed at Jason for not passing him the ball, and the coach told Chris to go shower—*now!* When Chris was gone, the coach asked, "What's with Chris, you guys?"

"Beats us, Mr. Connor. He sure is a pain!"

Fred Connor was concerned. Here was a kid who used to be a pretty good team member. Now he was sullen and uncooperative. What could be causing it?

He caught Chris before he left and called him into his office. "Chris, I think it's time we had a talk."

"Yeah? What about?"

"You. What's the matter?"

"Nothing."

"Come off it, Chris. You're not the same kid you were a month ago. You're angry, you're upset, and there must be a reason for it. I'm not here to lecture you but I'd like to help you if there's a problem. I've known you a long time and I think we can level with each other!"

Chris didn't know what to do. The guilt he felt over Tim was eating him up inside but if he told Mr. Connor what a rotten thing he'd done— "I've just got a lot of things on my mind."

"I can see that. Can you tell me about any of them?"

"It's the usual stuff—grades, parents—you know. And I've been kind of upset about Tim." Chris wasn't sure where that last sentence had come from. He hadn't meant to say it, but Mr. Connor seemed so interested, like he really cared.

"I can certainly understand that. All of us at school were upset when Tim died. Lots of us wonder if we could have done something to prevent it."

Chris sat up. "You do? I keep thinking the same thing."

"Chris, were you close to Tim?"

"Well, sort of. I mean, we spent some time together. He was pretty easy to be around. Didn't bug you too much."

"Is there something about him that bothers you?" Mr. Connors asked.

"Well...I've been thinking that I should have paid more attention to some of the things he did."

"What things?"

"Well, he gave me some stuff just before he died. Some books he collected that he knew I liked. I was thinking that maybe he was trying to tell me something."

"I suppose he might have been. Does that make a difference?"

"It bothers me! If I'd been paying attention maybe he wouldn't be dead!" Chris sounded really angry. But he also sounded scared.

Mr. Connor stayed very calm and ignored Chris's angry tone. "Do you feel guilty about that?"

"Sure I do. How would *you* like it if you thought you might have let someone die because you were too selfish to listen to him?"

So that's what the problem is, thought Mr. Connor. "Chris, I think I can understand how you feel. Just about every teacher who had Tim in class is wondering if they missed some clue that would have told them Tim was thinking about suicide. We all feel guilty that we maybe didn't pay enough attention. The trouble is, when Tim was alive, the things he said or did didn't have the meaning they have now."

"But he gave me those books! And I was so busy with my own problems, I didn't pay any attention!"

"Chris, we can *all* say we didn't pay enough attention! But you've got to remember that no one can be responsible for someone else's life. Sure, we'd all feel better if we were sure we'd done all we could for Tim. That's what's so bad about suicide—we'll never be able to feel that way! But you have to try not to blame yourself for something you didn't know anything about. When it happened, you didn't know those books were a final present. Give yourself a break, Chris."

"Thanks, Mr. Connor." Chris paused a moment. "I'll try, but I still wonder if—"

"So do we all, Chris. So do we all. Do me a favor. Think about what we've said. And promise me that if you need to talk about this some more you'll come to me. If I can't help you, I'll find someone who can."

"OK. You know, I didn't realize that other people might feel guilty too. In a way that makes things easier. Damn! I wish Tim hadn't done that!"

"Me too, Chris."

Anger

Anger is an emotion that can be a convenient substitute for other feelings: fear, guilt, helplessness. When someone commits suicide, it's easy to be mad at them for putting such a burden on us. It may help to remember that the first priority of a suicidal person is to end their emotional pain, not to increase ours.

Guilt

One of the most damaging aspects of suicide is the guilt felt by so many of the people who knew the person who died. And feelings of guilt can be overwhelming. Chris may think he didn't do enough to prevent Tim's death but he must understand that what he was aware of before Tim's suicide is different from what he knows now. He will have to try not to blame himself for things he didn't understand. He may find comfort in knowing that other people are wondering if they could or should have done something too. Even when someone does all he or she can to prevent it, a friend or relative may still commit suicide—and that is no one's fault. Like it or not, we can't *make* another person live.

CHAPTER FIVE
She Was Only Trying To Help

"Hi, Heather, how are you?"

"Terrible, thanks to you! You had no right to talk to my parents. I'll never forgive you for what you did!"

Stephanie heard Heather hang up. Why couldn't Heather understand that she'd been frightened? That she couldn't handle it? That she'd done it for Heather?

Stephanie and Heather had been best friends just about forever. Stephanie remembered their first day as freshmen in high school. Heather had called the night before. "Steph, what are you wearing tomorrow?"

"I thought I'd wear my new jeans and that striped shirt with my white belt. How about you?"

"I can't decide. Do you think a skirt would be too dressy?"

"Well...maybe. We don't want to be too dressed up or everybody'll know we're freshmen!"

"Yeah. I see what you mean. OK. I'll wear jeans too. Are you going to meet me at school? I don't want to go in by myself."

"You bet! I'll meet you at the side door at seven-thirty. And at lunch we can sit together."

"Great! It sure is nice to have a friend to lean on."

"I'll say. See you tomorrow."

Stephanie smiled a little, remembering how she and Heather always tried to help each other. They had spent hours on the phone, telling each other their troubles, from parents who didn't understand to boys they liked who didn't notice them. Now it looked as if Heather would never be her friend again. She thought back.

It must have been around Christmas that Heather had seemed to change. Stephanie had noticed that she seemed awfully quiet.

"Hey, Heather, do you want to go shopping at the mall tomorrow?"

"I don't think so, Steph. I can't get excited about Christmas this year."

"What? You like Christmas better than anybody I know!"

"I used to, but I just don't care very much this year."

"Heather—what's the matter?"

"Nothing, really. Just a lot of little things."

"Heather, this doesn't sound like you—you're always so happy!"

"I guess I got tired of being happy. I'll talk to you tomorrow."

I wonder what's bugging her, Stephanie thought. *Maybe she had a fight with her parents.* With "Miss Perfect" Debbie at home for the holidays, Heather would be having a hard time. It really bugged Steph that Heather's parents were always comparing Heather to her older sister. They thought Debbie was so wonderful and were always telling Heather to "be more like your sister." Sure, Debbie got good grades and was popular, but Steph thought she was kind of conceited.

Oh, well, she thought, *Heather'll get over whatever's bothering her.*

But she hadn't. Even after the holidays, Heather had been different and hadn't taken much interest in anything. Stephanie had decided she needed to find out what was going on.

"Heather, I'm coming over tonight and we're going to talk. I want to know what's wrong."

"Oh, Steph, it's nothing you can help with."

"Listen, I'm your best friend aren't I?"

"Yes."

"Well, best friends are supposed to listen and that's what I'm going to do. I'll see you about eight. And no arguments! OK?"

"Yeah."

Stephanie rang the doorbell right at eight o'clock. "Hi, Heather."

"Oh...hi, Steph." Heather had circles under her eyes. She looked like she hadn't been sleeping well—not like the old Heather who could sleep *anywhere.*

"Can we go up to your room?"

"I guess so."

The girls settled themselves and Stephanie jumped right in. "Listen, Heather, I know something's wrong and I want to help. Even if I can't actually do anything, I can at least listen. *Please* tell me what's wrong!"

Heather finally talked about how bad she had been feeling. No matter how hard she tried, she could never be as good as Debbie. She wasn't as smart, as pretty, or as popular, and never would be. She was so tired of always trying and failing. Maybe her parents would appreciate her more if she weren't around.

"I keep thinking how nice it would be to sleep forever," Heather said. "I read somewhere that when you freeze to death it doesn't really hurt or anything—you just get sleepy. I could just go outside when it's really cold and stay there until it's over. Or maybe I could get some pills—that wouldn't be bad. I bet my funeral would be really nice—lots of flowers and stuff."

Heather had a sort of dreamy look on her face as she talked, and Stephanie was scared.

I think she means what she's saying! Stephanie thought. *I have to do something . . . but* what?

Stephanie did her best to cheer up her friend. She used every argument she could think of to get Heather to understand that her problems wouldn't last forever. She tried to convince Heather to tell her parents how she felt, but she left the house feeling that she hadn't gotten very far. Even though she thought Heather's parents compared their children too much, Stephanie had always liked them. They loved Heather, she was sure. Maybe if she told them about Heather's feelings they would do something to help. They probably didn't even realize that Heather was in trouble. Yes, she was going to talk to them—they just *had* to understand.

A few days later, Stephanie worked up her courage and went to see Heather's mom. She told her about the conversation and said that she was worried about Heather but didn't know what to do. Heather's mother was really nice.

"Stephanie, I'm so glad you told me about this! Now, I don't want you to worry. Heather's father and I will get help for her. You did the right thing in telling us. Thank you!"

Steph was surprised that Heather wasn't in school the next day. She called Heather's house as soon as she got home. "Oh, Stephanie, dear, we've hospitalized her so that she can get help and won't be able to do anything foolish. She's seeing a psychiatrist who's very good. The doctor has had a lot of success with girls who are depressed, and she recommended that we put her in the hospital. Just to be safe. We don't know how long she'll be in the hospital but it shouldn't be more than a few weeks."

"Oh, Mrs. Fremont, did you have to put Heather in the hospital? Is she going to be OK?"

"We hope so, Steph. The doctor told us that hospitalization would be the most efficient way to treat Heather's case and we agreed." Mrs. Fremont hesitated "I don't know if we did the right thing. Heather is extremely angry right now, but the doctor says she'll get over that and that her anger is healthier than her depression. We were so frightened that she would hurt herself that we couldn't think of anything else to do."

In fact, Heather had been in the hospital for two months. She had written Stephanie one letter:

> Steph—I hope you're proud of yourself for ruining my life. I trusted you when I told you how I felt and instead of being my friend you went to my parents and they stuck me in here. Now everybody will think I'm crazy and I'll never be able to face the kids at school. You should have remembered that it's *my* life and I can do what I want with it. Don't *ever* try to talk to me again!
>
> Heather

Warning Signs

There are a number of warning signs of possible suicide. More than one of these signs, repeated over a period of time, indicates that suicide is being contemplated. In Heather's case, she had shown personality changes, difficulty in sleeping, and had talked about dying. It's important to take such changes seriously. For a full list of warning signs, see chapter one.

Risks

Very few people know what to do when they suspect that a friend is suicidal. Sometimes the choices available are difficult ones. Any choice involves certain risks: if they say and do nothing, the friend may try and succeed in committing suicide. On the other hand, if they tell someone else about their fears, their friend may become very angry. There was no way that Stephanie could tell for sure whether or not Heather was ready to take her life. If she had not acted, and Heather had committed suicide, Stephanie would have felt terribly guilty for not doing something to stop her.

Whether or not Heather's parents should have hospitalized her is a question we can't answer. Sometimes hospitalization is the only choice or the best choice. Eventually Heather may realize that Stephanie cared and was trying to help her. It comes down to this: would you rather have a live, possibly angry, friend— or a dead one?

CHAPTER SIX

That's the Kid Who Tried To Kill Himself

"Psst! See that kid in the blue shirt? He tried to kill himself!"

"Wow—what'd he do?"

"I don't know exactly, but he's been in the hospital for awhile and sees a shrink."

"Boy, he must be crazy!"

Jerry could have slugged those kids. That was his friend Greg they were talking about! How could they be so stupid! Sure, Greg had had problems and tried suicide, but he wasn't crazy. It was going to be hard enough for him to be back with his classmates without all that whispering behind his back.

Jerry walked up to Greg and said, "I'll meet you at the cafeteria at lunch. OK?"

Greg smiled and said, "Sure, that'll be great."

As usual, the cafeteria was wild at lunch—except where Jerry and Greg sat. It was pretty obvious that nobody was anxious to sit with Greg. Kids would glance at their table and quickly look around for another place to sit. When all other seats were taken, a couple of kids sat with them. They ate quickly and left. Jerry was embarrassed and angry, but he didn't know what to do. Greg ate with his head down, not saying anything. Finally, Jerry said, "Are you going to the game after school?"

Greg shook his head. "Nah, I've got a lot of work to catch up on."

"Well," Jerry said, "I'll see you at lunch tomorrow."

Jerry went to the game that afternoon and sat with a group of his friends. "How come you hang around with that weird kid?" Doug asked him.

"What weird kid?"

"You know—that guy Greg that tried to off himself."

"Listen," Jerry snapped, "I've known Greg a long time and he's a nice kid. Just because he's had some problems doesn't make him weird!"

"Ha! If you hang around with him, people are going to think you're weird too!"

Jerry tried to ignore what Doug had said, but he couldn't. Would people think he was "weird" if he stayed friends with Greg? How could he just dump Greg when he'd known him so long?

He decided to mention the problem to his mother—not straight out, but kind of subtly. "Mom, did you know Greg is back in school?"

"Yes, I talked with his mother just the other day. She was really pleased. How's he doing?"

"Well, he's kind of quiet, but OK, I guess."

"I'm glad. It's awfully tough to go back to junior high after something like this. Kids can be so cruel! I hope you're being nice to him."

"Oh, Mom."

Well, that didn't do much good, Jerry thought. *She just doesn't understand. All she can do is lecture.*

The rest of the week was the same story. Jerry made sure he ate lunch with Greg, but after school, Greg went home. The kids had stopped talking about Greg in front of Jerry, but he knew that they still discussed "the kid who tried to kill himself" when he wasn't around. Jerry didn't know exactly what to do. If he didn't have anything to do with Greg, he was letting both Greg and himself down. If he tried to get Greg together with his other friends they might dump *him.*

Fortunately, Jerry's older sister came home from college for a weekend visit. When she finally sat down to catch up on his news, he saw his chance.

"So, Jer, you don't sound so great. What's the matter?"

"Well, you know Greg?"

"Sure. What about him?"

"Well, you know he tried to commit suicide a few months ago?"

"Yeah. Mom told me."

"Well, he was in the hospital a while and now he's back at school, and it's really hard."

"What's hard?"

"Well, I still like him, but a lot of the kids say he's weird, and everybody kind of avoids him."

"Oh—I get it. They think he's crazy or something—right?"

"Right."

"And?"

"And I still want to be friends with him, but if I do, I can lose all my other friends because they'll think I'm weird too." Jerry watched Cindy anxiously. She always seemed to know what to do, and he was counting on her.

Cindy was quiet for a minute. She wanted to help. She could imagine how difficult a situation like this could be. "What do you want to do, Jer?"

"That's the problem. I don't know."

"Look—the real problem is trying to handle this alone. Do you have any friends who'd be willing to help you—I mean is there anyone else who'd be willing to accept Greg?"

"Well...maybe if I talk to some of the guys, they would be." Jerry thought for a few minutes. "You know, Sis, it's worth a try. I sure don't have anything to lose."

That night, Jerry called his friend Bill. "Hey, Bill, I need to talk to you. You know Greg, don't you?"

"Sure. He's the kid who tried to kill himself."

"Well, you know he just got out of the hospital, and most of the kids won't have anything to do with him. I've known Greg a long time, and I'd really like to help him, but I can't do it alone. Will you help me?"

"Are you nuts? He's got to be crazy to have done what he did. I'm not hanging out with a freak!"

"Bill, listen to me! He's not crazy! He had a lot of problems—haven't you ever had any?"

"Yeah. But not like him."

"Greg just had more problems than most and didn't know how to handle them. But now he has one *big* problem. Remember that time when the guys got mad at you and wouldn't let you hang around with us?"

"That was different."

"It wasn't *that* different! You were really bummed and if it hadn't been for a couple of us sticking up for you, you *still* wouldn't be hanging around with us! How do you think Greg feels? He used to be friends with us, and now nobody'll touch him with a ten-foot pole! He's not crazy and he's not weird, he's just alone." Jerry took a deep breath. "Now, are you willing to help?"

"What would I have to do?"

"Nothing much. Let's see if he'll go to the game tomorrow. If he says 'yes,' then you sit with us. I'm going to try to get a couple other guys to do the same."

"I suppose that's OK," Bill said, "but you'd better get somebody else to go along, or it's no deal!"

After a lot of arguing, Jerry finally managed to get Jim and Zach to go along with his plan. The next morning Jerry saw Greg before school.

"Hey, Greg, how about coming to the game today?"

"Gee, I don't know. I really have a lot to do."

"Look, Greg," Jerry said, "I know you tried to commit suicide, but that's over now. The sooner you show that you're OK, the sooner everybody will accept you. Now, Bill and I and a couple other guys really want you to go to the game. Will you do it?"

Greg said, "I know you're trying to be nice, but I don't think it'll work. Everybody thinks there's something wrong with me. If I show up at the game they'll just whisper and snicker, and I'll feel like a jerk. I just don't want to face that."

"Greg, I understand how you feel, but if you're not going to go half-way, nothing's ever going to change! I know it's hard, but you've got to give this a try."

Greg stared at Jerry. "Well, I guess if you guys are willing to do this, I owe it to you to do it—but I still don't think it'll help."

Myths

People fear what they don't understand. It's easy for the myth to persist that people who try suicide are insane. In fact, very few of those who attempt suicide are "crazy." The most common characteristic of suicidal people is emotional pain. Any young person who seriously considers ending his or her life *hurts* inside. They can't imagine anyone hurting as they do and what they want most is to make that pain go away. Their thoughts may be something like this:

"Everything bad happens to me."

"Things are never going to get better."

"I can't do anything about it."

After a Suicide Attempt

Nobody likes being an outcast. Young people who have attempted suicide will be very uneasy about how friends and classmates may behave toward them. If you want to help, don't ignore this person. Treat him or her as you do your other friends. Let this person choose whether or not to talk about what happened. Remember that suicidal feelings are not a permanent emotional state. If the depression that caused the suicidal feelings has been treated, the person will be ready to take up his or her life again.

CHAPTER SEVEN
What'll I Say?

The funeral had been two weeks ago and Sarah still hadn't seen Michelle's family. She was afraid. After all, she'd been Michelle's best friend. Michelle's mom and dad probably hated her—she hadn't been able to help. How could a best friend not know what was going to happen? Would Michelle's family ever believe that she really hadn't known that Michelle was going to kill herself? Even if they did, wouldn't they feel like they never wanted to see her again? Wouldn't she bring back all kinds of unhappy memories for them?

Sarah had been stunned when she found out that Michelle was dead. She still couldn't believe it. She'd begun to realize that she would never know why Michelle had committed suicide, and that she'd always wonder. She still hadn't gotten over being angry with Michelle for causing so much unhappiness for other people.

Sarah's mom and dad had explained that the anger was part of grieving and that eventually she would remember the good times with Michelle.

But what about Michelle's family? They'd been like a second family to Sarah. She'd spent as much time at their house as she had at her own. Would she ever be able to see them again without causing a lot of unhappiness?

Sarah sighed as she got ready for bed. She couldn't stop worrying about it. She just didn't know what to do.

Sarah's mom knocked and came into the bedroom. "I just wanted to talk with you for a few minutes. Is that all right?"

"Sure, Mom."

"Sarah, I know you haven't been over to see the Johnsons since the funeral. Is that something you want to do?"

"I just don't know, Mom. I feel like I should, but I'm afraid of what might happen."

"What do you mean?"

"Won't the Johnsons blame me for not knowing that Michelle was suicidal? I mean, I was her best friend and if anybody should have known, I should. Maybe they'll think I should've done something . . . or have paid more attention to how Michelle was feeling . . . I just don't know!"

"Honey, do you feel that you could have done something to prevent what Michelle did?"

"I don't think so, Mom. Michelle never said anything to me about killing herself. She was a little more quiet than usual, but that's all. She never said anything about suicide. I talked to some other friends and nobody knew she was so unhappy."

"Sometimes people don't let anybody else know what they're thinking, Sarah, and even if they do, there may not be any way to stop them from taking their lives. I'm glad that you don't feel responsible for Michelle's death." She sighed. "I don't know how Michelle's parents are feeling right now. It's so hard to lose a child, especially this way. But they've always loved you and I don't think they'd blame you. I guess what you have to decide is if you have the courage to go see them when you don't know exactly how they're going to react. If you decide you want to visit them, I'll be happy to go with you, if that will help."

"Thanks, Mom. I guess I just need to think about it a little more."

Sarah had always felt that it was better to face up to difficult decisions than to avoid them. It seemed important for her to see the Johnsons sooner or later and she decided that sooner would be better.

A few days after her conversation with her mother, Sarah called Mrs. Johnson and asked if she could come over. Michelle's mother said yes.

"Do you want me to go with you?" asked Sarah's mother.

"I think I need to do this by myself, Mom."

Sarah was still frightened as she knocked at the Johnsons' door. Mr. Johnson answered.

"Hello, Sarah, it's good to see you."

"Thanks, Mr. Johnson, it's good to see you, too."

"Come in. Lydia's in the living room."

Both Mr. and Mrs. Johnson looked tired. Lydia Johnson gave Sarah a hug and asked her to sit down. There was an awkward silence. Sarah decided that she would say what was on her mind. "I've been so scared to come to see you. I've been afraid that you'd blame me for what happened to Michelle."

"Oh, Sarah, why would you think something like that?" Mr. Johnson exclaimed.

"I was Michelle's best friend. I was afraid you'd think I should have been able to stop her!"

Mrs. Johnson had tears in her eyes. "But Sarah, we were her *parents* and we couldn't stop her. How could we possibly blame you?"

Mr. Johnson cleared his throat and spoke to Sarah. "You know, Sarah, at first, after Michelle died, we asked ourselves a lot of questions. It seemed hard to believe that nobody knew she was going to do this, especially her mother and me. We'll probably always wonder if we could have saved her and that's something we'll have to live with. But we know it won't do any good to blame ourselves or anyone else for Michelle's death. We can only hope that we can go on living our lives. We'd give anything to have Michelle back but that's not going to happen. For everybody's sake we *all* have to go on living. We won't ever forget Michelle. We just hope that some day we'll be able to think about the wonderful times we all had together. And you were part of those good times. We don't want to lose you too!"

Sarah's eyes filled with tears. She hadn't realized until this moment how badly she needed the Johnsons not to blame her for Michelle's death. Somewhere in the back of her mind she was afraid that she'd missed a clue somewhere that would have told her what Michelle was going to do. She knew that it would take her a long time to forgive herself for not knowing, but it was going to be easier if the Johnsons didn't hate her.

When she got home, her mother was waiting for her. "Are you all right, honey?"

"Oh, Mom, the Johnsons were so nice to me! I feel so bad about Michelle!"

"I know you do, honey. We all do. We'll all just have to do our best to keep going. It'll take a long time to get over it."

Sarah made it a point to go see the Johnsons regularly. She believed that sharing the sadness of Michelle's death made them all feel a little better. As time went on they were able to talk more easily.

"I still wonder if I could've done anything different so Michelle would be alive today," Sarah said one evening when she was visiting the Johnsons.

"I think we'll all wonder about that for a long time to come," Mrs. Johnson said. "But it won't do any good. We can always say 'if only,' or 'what if,' but it won't change anything. Michelle was apparently a very unhappy girl. Even if we'd been aware of that, it might not have changed anything. I know how you feel because Frank and I ask ourselves the same questions. But we're learning to live with what happened. We'll never be the same as we would have been if this hadn't happened but we _will_ survive."

Sarah, too, was healing. She still thought about Michelle a lot, but not every minute as she'd done right after Michelle had died. There were even times when she and the Johnsons would talk about the good times they'd had. "Remember that time we wanted to spend the night in a tent in your back yard? You helped us put up the tent and then we roasted marshmallows over the charcoal grill because we couldn't have a camp fire?"

Lydia Johnson laughed. "What I remember best are the ghost stories we all told. If I remember correctly, mine were the scariest."

"Now just a minute, Lydia," Mr. Johnson said. "I thought mine were the best."

"Oh, I don't know," Sarah argued. "It seems to me that Michelle and I told one together and you two couldn't wait to get into the house where it would be safe!"

Everyone laughed. "You may be right, Sarah, because I remember that Frank and I nearly jumped out of our skins when you girls came in to tell us that it was too cold to sleep outside."

Sarah smiled. It was good to be able to talk about the past without crying. There would always be an empty spot with Michelle gone, but talking about her helped. And being together with the Johnsons seemed to help them all get used to life without Michelle.

After a Completed Suicide

When a young person commits suicide, the grief felt by family, friends, and associates is enormous. Talking with other people who share the loss can help. Sarah's fears about being blamed for Michelle's death were groundless, but that is not always the case. Particularly in suicide, it's easy to decide that someone could or should have done something to prevent the act. Some families might blame a friend—or each other; some friends might blame the parents—or each other. Fortunately for Sarah, the Johnsons were sensitive enough to understand that Sarah was hurting too, and that nothing would be gained by blaming her and adding to her grief.

It may take years for families in which there has been a teen suicide to recover from the tragedy. Each family will do its grieving in its own way. There is no specific time at which family members suddenly "recover." The important thing is that they have an opportunity to express their pain in ways that are acceptable to *them*. Being able to talk with other people who have been affected by the suicide can help a family get through the most difficult parts of its grief. No one will ever forget what happened. With time we can hope that the pain of the past will lessen and that the family will live in the present and look to the future.

CHAPTER EIGHT

Choices and Resources

What To Do

If you suspect that a friend may be considering suicide, the first and most important thing for you to do is not to keep that information a secret. It's hard to betray a friend who has asked you to keep what he or she has told you is a secret, but when your friend's life may be at stake, you MUST involve an adult immediately. This is not to say that an adult is able to be a better friend, but adults are able to help you and your friend find assistance. You must also have someone else to talk to, someone who can share the burden of your friend's pain with you.

If you have noticed some of the warning signs of suicide in a friend, one of the best ways to assess the immediacy of danger is to ask questions. These questions can show that you care about this person as well as give you some information about what is going on in your friend's mind. Some are:

Why are you so unhappy?
Has anything happened to make you feel so unhappy?
Does anyone else know the way you feel?
Have you thought about harming yourself?
Have you thought about how you might do this?
What would make things better for you?
What can I do to help you right now?

If you think your friend is in danger, it is very important not to leave him or her alone. If you can't stay with your friend, arrange for other people to take turns being with him or her. Being all alone can trigger, or make possible, a suicide attempt.

If you need a little time in order to get your friend professional help, you can try making a "contract" with him or her. In other words, you get your friend to agree not to do anything until he or she has talked with you or met with you. This kind of agreement will give you time to involve adults in the situation.

What Happens When People Get Professional Help

Suicidal feelings develop over time. And it takes time to understand those feelings. Most people who are so depressed that they think about suicide will need professional help to recover. This help involves discovering what can be done to lessen the emotional pain, and to reach a better understanding of the experiences that contributed to the problem. A large part of professional help involves creating an atmosphere in which the patient can express his or her feelings freely, so that the intensity of those feelings diminishes. People in treatment may go through some changes as they work on their problems—they may discover that they are very angry, or that they resent some of the people in their lives. They may need to change parts of their lives, including relationships with family and friends, in order to survive. They can begin to find more positive and less destructive ways to cope with their feelings as they recognize what those feelings truly are.

People To Talk To

In any community there are a number of resources available to deal with a potential suicide. If the first person or place you approach is not helpful, try again—and again—until you find someone who can help. Many young people feel awkward about approaching the troubled teen's parents directly. They are afraid the parents will be angry or will not listen. That might be true of some parents, but there are many other adults who might be willing to help. Among them are: your own parents, your older brothers or sisters, your friend's older brothers or sisters, teachers, counselors, clergy, family doctors, and adult friends.

In addition, there may be local agencies who have experience in this area. Some of the organizations to contact might be: a youth center, the police department (many of these now have social workers on their staff), a hospital emergency room, a mental health clinic, a family service organization, or a crisis hotline center.

If you are not sure what is available in your community, ask around. Or, look in the yellow pages of the phone book, or under "suicide" or "suicide prevention" in the white pages. This is a starting point for finding the kind of help you need. At the end of this book we have included a list of books and movies which may be helpful. If you want to learn more, your local library will undoubtedly have listings of what is available. Don't be afraid to ask the librarian for help in finding what you are looking for.

A Concluding Thought

Young people who choose suicide see no easing of their pain in the future. If we can offer them hope, they may choose to live instead of to die.

Reference Materials

Books—Non-Fiction

Alvarez, A. *The Savage God: A Study of Suicide.* New York: Random House, 1972

Friedman, Myra. *Buried Alive: The Biography of Janis Joplin.* New York: William Morrow, 1973

Giffin, Mary and Felsenthal, Carol. *A Cry for Help.* New York: Doubleday & Co., 1983

Klagsbrun, Francine. *Too Young to Die: Youth and Suicide.* New York: Pocket Books, 1984

Mack, John E. and Hickler, Holly. *Vivienne: The Life and Suicide of an Adolescent Girl.* New York: NAL, 1982

Wechsler, James A. *In A Darkness.* New York: W.W. Norton, 1972

Books—Fiction

Green, H. *I Never Promised You A Rose Garden.* New York: Signet Books, 1964

Guest, J. *Ordinary People.* New York: Viking Press, 1976

Neufeld, J. *Lisa Bright and Dark.* New York: Signet Books, 1969

Peck, R. *Remembering The Good Times.* New York: Delacorte Press, 1985

Educational Films and Videotapes

Did Jenny Have To Die. Sunburst Communications, Room SJ6, 39 Washington Ave., Pleasantville, NY 10570; 1980; videotape

Suicide: But Jack Was a Good Driver. McGraw-Hill Training Systems, Box 641, 674 Via de la Valle, Del Mar, CA 92014; 1974; videotape or film

Suicide: It Doesn't Have to Happen. BFA Educational Media, 468 Park Ave. S., New York, NY 10016; 1976; videotape or film

Suicide: The Warning Signs. Centron Films, 65 East S. Water St., Chicago, IL 60601; 1982; videotape or film

Teen Suicide. MTI Teleprograms Inc., 108 Wilmot Rd., Deerfield, IL 60015; 1985; videotape or film

Teens Who Chose Life: The Suicidal Crisis. Sunburst Communications, Room SJ6, 39 Washington Ave., Pleasantville, NY, 10570; 1986; videotape

About the Authors

Janet Kolehmainen is Director of Education for LINKS—North Shore Youth Health Service in Northfield, Illinois. She has been active for many years in creating and presenting education programs on suicide prevention and other topics of concern to teenagers. She is a graduate of Wellesley College and now lives in Illinois with her husband and two teenage children. Her two older children attend college.

Sandra Handwerk holds a M.Ed. in Guidance and Counseling and a Ph.D. in Human Services. The past Executive Director of LINKS—North Shore Youth Health Service, she has counseled young people and their families since 1971. Dr. Handwerk is committed to the concepts of prevention through education and community-based prevention programs. A native of Pennsylvania, Dr. Handwerk now lives in Illinois with her daughters, Katie and Rebecca.